BE BRAVE!

AN ACTIVITY BOOK FOR YOUNG PEOPLE WHO SOMETIMES FEEL SCARED OR AFRAID

Kane Miller
A DIVISION OF EDC PUBLISHING

Kane Miller
A DIVISION OF EDC PUBLISHING

First American Edition 2019
Kane Miller, A Division of EDC Publishing

© 2018 Studio Press
Written by Dr. Sharie Coombes, Child, Family & Adult Psychotherapist,
Ed.D, MA (PsychPsych), DHypPsych(UK), Senior QHP, B.Ed.
Edited by Frankie Jones
Illustrated by Katie Abey
Designed by Rob Ward

First published in the UK in 2018 by Studio Press,
an imprint of Bonnier Books UK

For information contact:
Kane Miller, A Division of EDC Publishing
PO Box 470663
Tulsa, OK 74147-0663
www.kanemiller.com
www.edcpub.com
www.usbornebooksandmore.com

Library of Congress Control Number: 2018942400

Printed in China
6 7 8 9 10

ISBN: 978-1-61067-861-2

BE BRAVE!

THIS BOOK BELONGS TO

_ _ _ _ _ _ _ _ _ _

WELCOME TO BE BRAVE!

We all feel afraid from time to time. This fun activity book is a great way to get you thinking and talking about the things that bother you, so you can get on with being you and get back to enjoying life.

Author
DR. SHARIE COOMBES
Child and Family Psychotherapist

Doing these activities will help you to feel braver, understand your feelings, make choices about how to react, talk to others about your worries (if you want to), and grow in courage, confidence and positivity. You could use this book in a quiet, comfortable place where you can think and where you feel relaxed. It's up to you which pages you do. You might do a page a day, if that's what you want, or you can complete lots of pages at once. You can start anywhere in the book and even come back to a page many times. There are no rules!

Sometimes things that worry us feel so big that we start to believe nothing will help, but there is always a solution to every problem. Nothing is so big that it can't be sorted out or talked about, even if it feels that way at the time. You could show some of these activities to important people in your life to help you to explain how you are feeling and what is upsetting you. You can always talk to an adult you trust at school or at home, or ask an adult to take you to the doctor for support to sort out any problems.

Lots of children need a bit of extra help every now and then, and here are two organizations you can turn to if you don't want to talk to people you know. They have talked to thousands of children with every imaginable problem and will know how to help you.

CRISIS TEXT LINE

Serves anyone, in any type of crisis, providing access to free, 24/7 support.
Connect with a trained crisis counselor to receive free, 24/7 crisis support via text message. Text HELLO to 741741

www.crisistextline.org

NATIONAL SUICIDE PREVENTION LIFELINE

24/7, free and confidential support for people in distress. Call free or chat online. No matter what problems you're dealing with, whether or not you're thinking about suicide, if you need someone to lean on for emotional support or are worried about a friend or loved one call the Lifeline.
www.suicidepreventionlifeline.org
1-800-273-8255

THE TURTLE, THE MOUSE AND ME!

Billions of brain cells work together to make up your remarkable brain, which helps you to plan, learn and understand. It's also responsible for every emotion and feeling you have.

SCARED

PANICKY

Emotions happen suddenly, causing a burst of chemicals to pump throughout your body. Feelings are what you notice in your body because of emotions. Fear, panic and phobia are some difficult feelings you may recognize.

PHOBIA

You might get flutters and butterflies when you're afraid. Your heart and stomach have brain cells, too.

THE GREAT NEWS IS THAT YOU CAN BREAK THIS HABIT AND LEARN TO DO THINGS DIFFERENTLY, FEEL MORE COURAGEOUS AND GET BACK IN CONTROL.

FREEZE, FIGHT, FLIGHT

Surrounded by hungry wild animals, our ancestors needed to be ready for anything. Their brains had to create feelings of fear to keep them alert and safe.

They learned to freeze and then run away from or fight off the threat. Nowadays, our brains don't need to be as cautious, so this ancient habit gets in our way.

Your brain has three parts that work both separately and as a team.

TINY TURTLE-BRAIN

This ancient part of your brain controls your vital functions like heart rate, breathing, body temperature and balance.

We share this part with all animals, even reptiles.

MOUSE-BRAIN

Mammals developed this part a long time ago. It's responsible for fearful feelings that make us avoid scary things, feel panicky or develop phobias.

ME-BRAIN

Your me-brain makes you who you are. It learns, develops language, thinks and gives you your imagination.

It can be taught to take control and help you react differently to scary things.

Fear, panic and phobia are **NOT** forever.
YOU can get rid of them and it's easier than you think!
Do the activities to find out what you can achieve. **HAVE FUN!**

MY STARTLE SIGNS

Everyone finds it hard to be brave sometimes.

When you're afraid, your body reacts in ways that feel very uncomfortable.

HELP ME!

Relax – it's just your tiny turtle-brain getting in a flap, calling on mouse-brain and me-brain to help out while it stays in its shell.

THIS IS ME

Add words, pictures and patterns to this page to show your turtle-brain's startle signs and express what it's like for you when you're afraid or panicky. Look at the next page for some ideas.

BE BRAVE!
TURTLE TAMER!

Challenge yourself to learn and practice the **BE BRAVE!** steps every time you're afraid or in a panic.

Want to BE BRAVE? You can tame your startled turtle-brain and teach it to feel safer, calmer, and braver.

Put a check in this grid every time you tame your turtle-brain.

BE AWARE of the startle signs in your body.

ENCOURAGE turtle-brain to fold into its shell.

BREATHE slowly and deeply five times.

RELAX your me-brain to deal with the problem and...

ASK mouse-brain to comfort turtle-brain.

VISUALIZE yourself acing this.

ENJOY being brave!

Deep breaths feel like gentle waves lapping on a beach, relaxing your turtle-brain.

Can you learn the BE BRAVE! steps by heart?

What's on your mind, tiny turtle?

MOUSE NOUS!

What could you say to the mouse to keep it feeling courageous?

Your mouse-brain jumps into action as quick as a flash, but it is pretty smart and you can easily train it to be brave with a few soothing strokes every day.

I'll help you to get through this.

You'll soon feel OK again.

To help the mouse feel safe and protected, draw it somewhere to shelter, something to keep it comfortable, and something to do.

I've got this.

ALL OF ME

Even if it doesn't always feel like it,
your fears are just a small part of you.
You are SO much bigger than your fears.

Put one or two of your biggest fears in the middle shapes, then fill the rest with all the things you enjoy doing, the people you love and who love you, the things you're good at, great memories you have, things you've achieved, nice things people have said about you and anything else you can think of.

ZEN TRIANGLES

Triangle breathing is a great way to calm your whole brain and put you back in control.

Run your finger along the sides of a triangle as you breathe in, hold and smile, then breathe out.

Do this on as many of the triangles as you want. You can even use the palm of your hand if you run out of triangles!

1. DEEP, SLOW BREATH IN

2. HOLD AND SMILE

3. DEEP, SLOW BREATH OUT

Why not color in or decorate some triangles with Zentangle patterns?

Try breathing out for longer than you breathe in.

AWESOME ME-BRAIN

Your me-brain is awesome!

Your skills, interests and talents come from your me-brain.

Add the things your me-brain can do or knows to this page.

Ask others for ideas if you get stuck.

Dear me-brain,

Thank you for everything.

You're awesome!

Love,
the rest of me X

CAN YOUR ME-BRAIN DO ANY OF THESE THINGS?

Read, write, dance, sing, remember, play sports, challenge yourself, knit, recite times tables, speak French, play chess, skip.

LET ME COUNT THE WAYS

Use this page to write down all the ways your life is going to be better now that you're learning to BE BRAVE! What will make the biggest difference to you?

Who will be the first person to notice the changes?

Be super creative with colors, crazy writing or whatever you like.

THE TREE OF LIFE

Color in the figure that's in the same place as you are now and write down the date and time.

Life's challenges are easier on some days and harder on others, depending on how you're feeling.

Where are you right now in the tree of life?

Come back to this later today, and over the days and weeks ahead, and fill in where you are each time.

LION OR HAMSTER?

Sometimes fear tricks us into believing something is like a terrifyingly fierce lion, when really it's just a timid hamster.

Both have teeth, fur, claws, tails and shiny eyes, but one is cute and no threat to you, while the other is much scarier.

We often forget to check the facts and it's easy to mistake the hamster for a lion when the turtle-brain and mouse-brain are in charge.

Draw or write down the things that scare you in these boxes.

__/10

HAMSTER ☐
LION ☐

Say how much each one bothers you by scaling it from 1 to 10, where 1 is completely fine and 10 is the most terrifying thing you can imagine.

__/10

HAMSTER ☐
LION ☐

__/10

HAMSTER ☐
LION ☐

When you've scaled your fears, look again using your me-brain and mark whether it's really just a hamster or if it actually feels like a lion to you.

___/10   HAMSTER ☐
          LION ☐

___/10   HAMSTER ☐
          LION ☐

___/10   HAMSTER ☐
          LION ☐

How many are hamsters?
How many are lions?
Which lion is the fiercest?

___/10   HAMSTER ☐
          LION ☐

How many are hamsters? ☐

How many are lions? ☐

Ask your friends or loved ones to tell you about their lions and hamsters.

HELLO, SUNSHINE!

Some people are like sunshine. Spend more time with these people.

Draw in the faces of your sunshine people and write down their names.

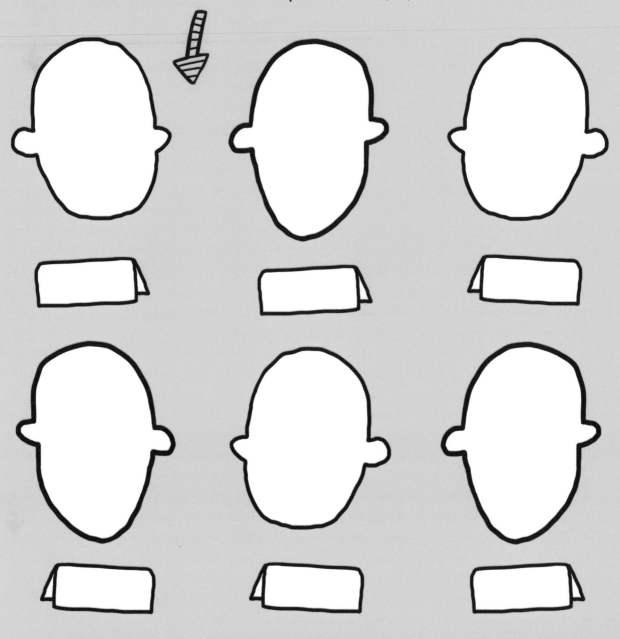

YOU DID IT!

Fill in these notes to remind yourself of times when something felt too difficult, but you were brave and did it anyway.

Why not write these down on sticky notes and put them up somewhere so that you'll see them every day?

GO, ME!

FEEL THE FEAR AND DO IT ANYWAY!

BRAVE SAVES THE DAY!

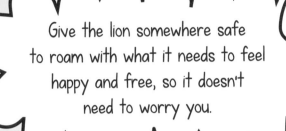

Give the lion somewhere safe to roam with what it needs to feel happy and free, so it doesn't need to worry you.

Send some of your other lions to this new home to form a pride – don't forget to label their tails.

MEMORY PUZZLE

Memory is stored in separate parts of your brain in tiny fragments.

People often remember the same event in a slightly different way, depending on what was important to them.

Memories are not exact recordings.

Think of a fun time you had with someone and draw or stick a photo of it here. Write down two things you remember about it.

Ask the other person to remember two things about the same event without letting them see what you've written. Are there any differences?

I CAN BE BRAVE!

Draw a situation or something that gets you feeling afraid or panicky.

Add lots of detail to your picture.

I'M BIGGER THAN YOU!

Remember to enjoy how it feels to **BE BRAVE!**

I CAN ASK FOR HELP.

Take your time to notice every part of your picture as you color it in carefully. You can stop to do triangle breathing as often as you need to. Keep going until your whole mind feels peaceful when looking at the picture.

Now add words all around your picture to remind yourself that it can't hurt you here. Put that old fear in its place and tell it you're no longer afraid – you're brave.

SAME
DIFFERENCE

Even when you're not feeling OK,
many parts of you are still 100% OK.

Draw yourself feeling afraid.
What are your startle signs?

Now draw the parts of you that are fine.

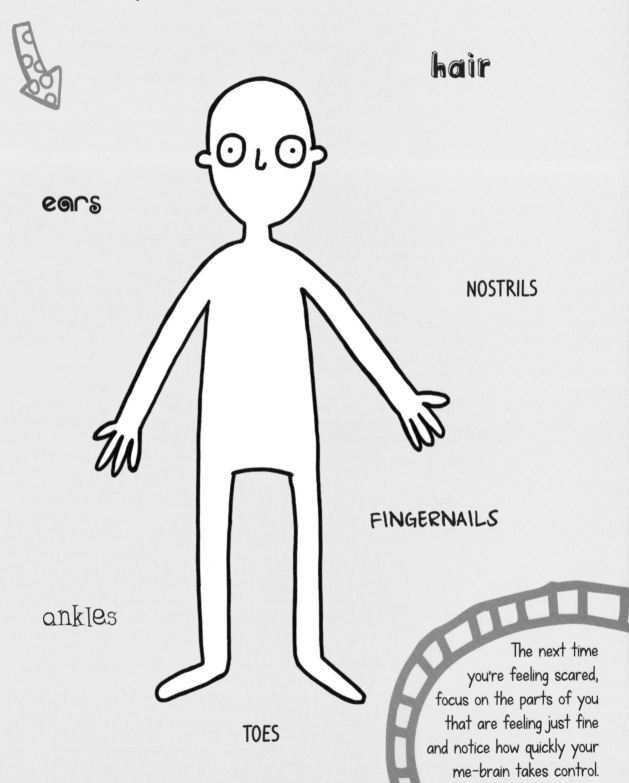

hair

ears

NOSTRILS

FINGERNAILS

ankles

TOES

The next time you're feeling scared, focus on the parts of you that are feeling just fine and notice how quickly your me-brain takes control.

SOMETHING FISHY

Nothing calms the mind like watching fish swimming. Why not make your own aquarium jar to help you to unwind? Ask an adult to help you with this activity.

You will need:

- A large jar with a lid
- Aquarium gravel or small stones
- Aquarium plant from a pet store
- Plastic fish or plastic sea creatures
- Small seashells
- Pitcher of water with blue food coloring or ink and/or glitter
- Hot glue, to be used by an adult only

Put the plant into the jar before the gravel; ask an adult to glue the plant in place.

Ask an adult to add some glue to the bottom of the jar and fill with gravel. Make sure the gravel is stuck down!

Make sure to cover all sides of the plant base to about one to two inches.

Allow the glue to dry and trim the plant so it fits.

Now add your plastic fish or sea creatures. Don't use any live creatures!

Next, pop in a few seashells.

Fill the pitcher with water, which you can color with a few drops of blue ink or food coloring, or add some glitter – or you can leave it clear.

Slowly fill the jar with the water to half an inch from the top and screw the lid on tightly.

Keep your jar upright.

You could seal the lid with hot glue, but ask an adult to help you with that.

Shake, watch and enjoy!

WHAT'S IN A NAME?

Your name is important to both yourself and to others who love you.

Slowly spell out your name with one finger onto the palm of your hand – it might be your full name, your nickname or just your first name. Now do this on each of your fingers, too.

Shake things up and try this with a friend or grown-up. Spell out your name really slowly on the palm of their hand and then ask them to spell theirs on your hand.

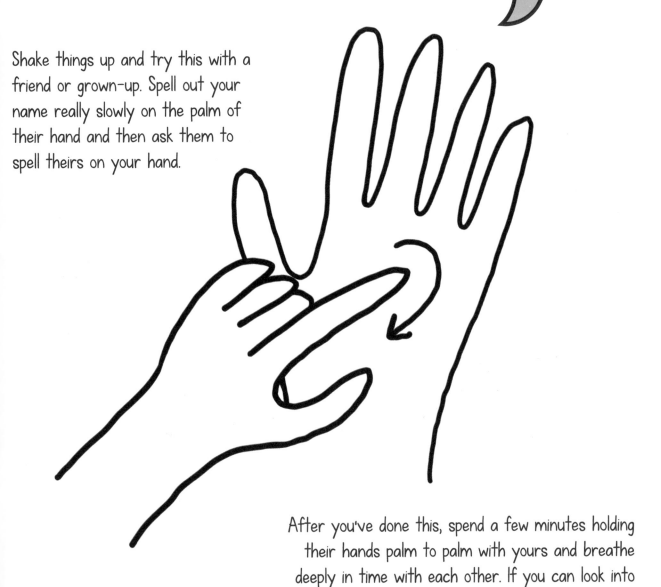

After you've done this, spend a few minutes holding their hands palm to palm with yours and breathe deeply in time with each other. If you can look into each other's eyes while you breathe, even better.

BIG POND, LITTLE FISH

Who belongs in your safe and sunny pond?
Turn your loved ones into underwater creatures and start splashing around together.

Make sure you include everyone
who supports you and helps you,
even pets and favorite soft toys.

COLOR THIS IN HOWEVER YOU LIKE.

I AM
NOT
ALONE

PET ROCKS

A pet rock family is easy to take care of, and can give you hours of fun and good company! Want to make up stories or plays for your pet rock family? GO FOR IT!

Start by taking a stroll with an adult along the beach, in the park, in the woods or even in your backyard.

Look for interesting natural objects to use to create your pets, along with five or six smooth stones or pebbles that fit in the palm of your hand.

Take a plastic bag to use to scoop up some feathers, leaves or whatever catches your eye.

It's important you don't pick any plants or berries and that you don't go anywhere that's on private property.

If you prefer, you could use craft materials as well as or instead of natural objects.

Clean your objects with dish soap and warm water, then dry them completely with paper towel.

Gather the rest of your supplies:

- Paint
- Markers
- Googly eyes
- Craft glue
- Ribbon
- Beads
- Buttons
- Pom-poms
- Scissors
- Paintbrushes

You can leave your rocks natural, paint them or use markers to decorate them.

Use your supplies and natural objects to add faces, wings, spots, stripes, or anything you like!

When you make your pet rocks, show their individual personalities and qualities by how you decorate them.

MAKE SURE YOU ASK AN ADULT TO HELP YOU WITH ANY CUTTING OR GLUING.

If you have a piece of wood, you could give them a base to sit on.

THROW SOME SHAPES

TURN UP THE MUSIC AND DANCE!

Grab a friend or just do it by yourself.

Circles, squares, triangles – any shapes you can make with your body.

Use your arms, hands, hips, legs, and feet – in fact, use every part of you!

GO CRAZY – NO ONE IS WATCHING!

Dancing to music is great when you're feeling afraid.

It helps get rid of fear quickly and will give you lots more **NATURAL ENERGY.**

YOU'LL FEEL:

- less stressed
- less tired
- less anxious
- less frustrated
- more comfortable
- more able to concentrate
- more able to sleep well
- more positive

AND YOU'LL HAVE HEAPS MORE FUN!

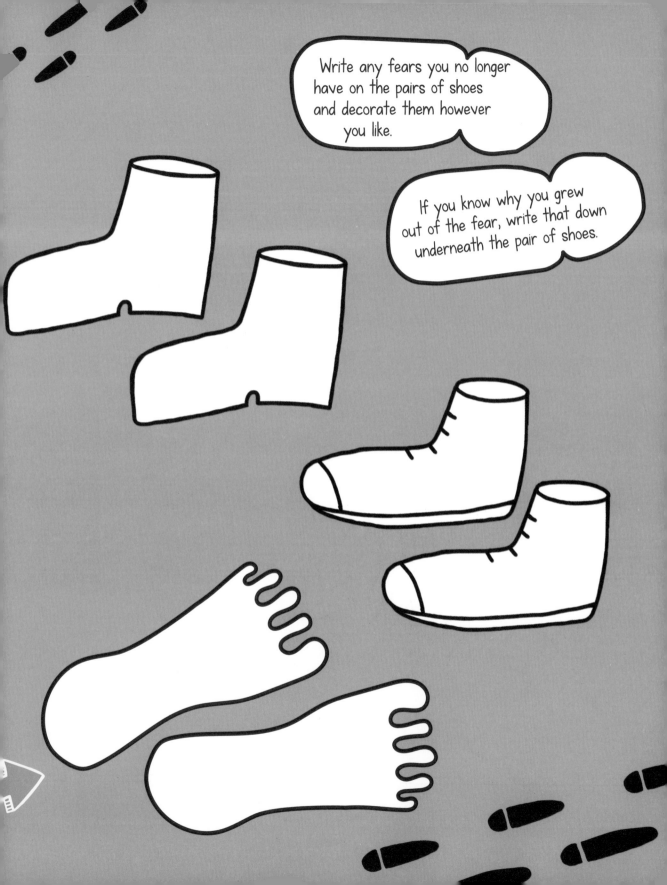

FOSSILS

One day, today's fears will be fossils.

Teaching your me-brain to be in
charge helps this to happen even more quickly,
leaving you free to get on with enjoying life.

Bury your fears in these rocks and watch them turn into fossils.
What will future fossil hunters notice about your old fears?

I AM SAFE

COLOR THIS IN

Write or draw the people and things that make you feel safe on the umbrella.

HELP!

It's really hard to ask for help, but you get better at it with practice.

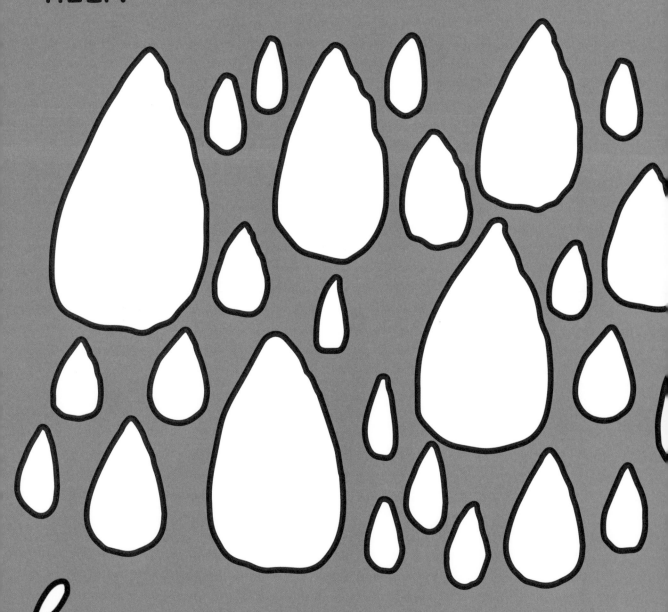

Fill each of these raindrops with a time you could have asked for help.
Spend a minute or two on each raindrop and imagine who you'd ask,
how you'd ask and what might have gone differently.

Color in the raindrop once you've done this.
You can keep coming back to this activity as you think of things.

WORRY TIME

Ask an adult at home to do this activity with you. If there's more than one adult, they could take turns.

SET A TIME TO DO THIS FOR 10 MINUTES EVERY DAY FOR 10 DAYS.

During these 10 minutes, speak about your worries and fears and nothing else.

The adult should listen lovingly and not try to fix anything during this time (they can help you with it later).

If you run out of worries, just sit together chatting until the time is up.

After 10 minutes do 10 slow, deep breaths together while holding hands and looking directly into each other's eyes (you might giggle!).

Then have a 10-second hug.

Record your worry time on this grid with a check mark.

10 minutes

10 deep
breaths

10-second
hug

Here are some good ways to listen lovingly.
Which ones would you like your adult to use?

☑

☐ It's OK to be afraid.

☐ I can support you to BE BRAVE!

☐ I will help you work it out.

☐ I'm here for you.

☐ It's really hard for you right now.

☐ I'm listening.

☐ Tell me more about it.

☐ I hear you.

☐ It doesn't feel fair.

☐ I want to be here for you.

☐ This feeling will pass.

☐ You've got what it takes.

☐ I can see why that is scary for you.

☐ I'll stay close so we can sort that
out together when you're ready.

BUBBLE TIME

Draw yourself in the center bubble.
Make sure you look relaxed, happy and comfy.

Make the outside of your big bubble really thick and use your
favorite colors. Color inside the bubble if you want to.

The little bubbles are your fears. Color them, label them or leave them blank as you wish.

1. DEEP, SLOW BREATH IN
2. HOLD AND SMILE
3. DEEP, SLOW BREATH OUT

While doing triangle or slow, deep breathing, spend five minutes imagining the little bubbles coming toward you but not being able to get to you at all because you are safe and happy in the big bubble.

Make your bubble thicker if you need to.

You can pop the little bubbles when they've lost their power over you.

Write on the cheeky monkeys, in the order they happen, the different things you notice happening in your body when you get scared.

DOODLE ME

Get creative with some wacky doodles.

Don't think,
just draw!

BOX CLEVER

Fiddle your way out of fear! Find a box you can use for this next activity – maybe an old shoebox, lunch box or ice cream carton. Decorate it however you like.

Fill your box with items you like the feel of, and then you can fiddle with them whenever you need to relax or calm down.

Put anything you want into your box. Here are some ideas:

soft toys

Worry stones

MODELING CLAY

WASHCLOTH

fidget toys

Bubble wrap

RUBBER BANDS

STRESS BALL

Beads

Pom-poms

Friendship bracelets

HAND LOTION

If you are sometimes afraid at school, ask your teacher if you can have a box in your classroom.

IN THE NEWS

News stories about things that happen in the world often make people feel sad, anxious or confused. It's OK to have these feelings – you won't be the only one. Here's what to remember:

It's called NEWS because it's rare. These terrible things are on the news because they do not happen very often.

YOU ARE SAFE
Look around you right now. You're safe. Ask for a hug or a chat.

SHARE YOUR WORRIES
Talk about it with an adult you trust at home or school and share what's troubling you.

IT'S OK
Being sad, worried or angry about it is OK and normal.
Adults get sad and confused about these things, too.

COLOR IN THE NOTES AS YOU READ THEM.

DO SOMETHING FUN
Watch your favorite film, take a dog for a walk, play football with your friends, read some of your favorite books or do some pages of this book!

IT'S NOT THE WHOLE STORY
THE WORLD IS A GREAT PLACE AND SO MANY WONDERFUL THINGS HAPPEN EVERY DAY. LOOK FOR THE KIND PEOPLE WHO DO GENEROUS AND THOUGHTFUL ACTS TO HELP OTHERS.

LOTTO

Thinking about other people gives you less time to think about your own fears.
Cross off each act of kindness on this lotto game as you complete it.
When you've filled in the whole page, do something nice for yourself.

WRITE A NOTE TO SOMEONE YOU CARE ABOUT	THANK AN ADULT FOR SOMETHING AT HOME	HELP SOMEONE BEFORE THEY ASK	CLEAN UP AFTER YOURSELF
LET SOMEONE GO BEFORE YOU	PUSH SOMEONE'S CHAIR IN IF THEY FORGET	THANK AN ADULT FOR SOMETHING AT SCHOOL	HOLD A DOOR OPEN FOR SOMEONE
INVITE SOMEONE NEW TO PLAY AT RECESS	GIVE A COMPLIMENT	SAY HELLO TO SOMEONE NEW	THANK A FRIEND FOR SOMETHING
MAKE A CARD FOR YOUR FAVORITE PERSON	GIVE ANOTHER COMPLIMENT	HELP SOMEONE WHO HAS DROPPED SOMETHING	CLEAN UP AFTER SOMEONE ELSE, EVEN THOUGH IT'S NOT YOUR MESS

LAND ART

Go out into your backyard, a park, beach or school sports field with a friend or an adult.

Make sure someone knows where you are.

Make some land art on the ground using only natural things you find lying around.

You could use pieces of wood, acorns, seeds, shells, stones, leaves or anything that you don't have to pick.

Your picture can be really detailed or just a shape like a spiral, a heart, or whatever you like.

LEAVE YOUR WORK IN PLACE FOR PASSERSBY TO ENJOY.

Color in these pages and draw your land art here.
You could look at the work of artist Andy Goldsworthy for ideas.

FEED YOUR WARRIOR

Inside your me-brain there's a warrior who's already overcome lots of difficulties. The beliefs you have about yourself depend on which ones you feed. Let's feed your inner warrior!

YOGA – WARRIOR 1

Stand straight, then step forward with one leg, with the front knee bent and your back leg straight out behind you. Arch your back, stretching your arms and hands up to the sky. Look straight ahead.

SAY "I AM STRONG."

YOGA – WARRIOR 2

From Warrior I pose, stretch your arms out in front of you and turn your chest to one side. Keep one arm stretched forward, the other stretched behind you.

SAY "I AM POWERFUL."

YOGA – WARRIOR 3

From Warrior 2, bring both arms in front of you, straighten your front leg, lifting your back foot off the ground slightly. Open your arms for balance if needed.

SAY "I AM BRAVE."

You can also strengthen your turtle-brain and mouse-brain to be even more courageous.

TURTLE POSE

With your legs stretched to the sides and your knees bent, push your head and stomach forward, tucking your hands under your ankles.

SAY "I CHOOSE CALM."

MOUSE POSE

Kneel on the floor, feet together. Rest your chest on your thighs and your chin on your knees, with your arms and hands by your sides, palms up.

SAY "I AM SAFE AND PROTECTED."

Stand up to those lions with this...

...LION POSE.

Kneel on the floor, feet together. With your hands on your knees or on the floor in front, arch your back. Lift your head and stretch out your tongue as if you're roaring for three seconds,

THEN SAY "I AM JUST AS FIERCE AS YOU."

KINDNESS COOKIES

Give someone a kindness cookie. See how good it makes them feel and how great it makes YOU feel!

WHO WILL YOU GIVE YOUR KINDNESS COOKIES TO?

Draw around the top of a cup to make a circle.

Here are some ideas, but you can write whatever you want:

YOU ROCK.

I LOVE YOU.

Write a tasty message
on it and cut it out.

YOU
ROCK

Write their name
on the other side.

Color it in and stick
glitter or sequins
on if you want.

YOU'RE SO SWEET.

YOU'RE SO BRAVE.

YOU CAN DO GREAT THINGS.

YOU'RE MY FRIEND.

Make a "Wanted" poster, so others can help you catch one
of your fears and get it out of the way for good.

WANTED!

GUILTY OF...

....

REWARD...

ABRACADABRA

If you had a magic wand and you could perform a miracle with it right now, what one thing would you change?

What is better now that you've changed it? Who will benefit?

Who will be the first to notice that things have changed?

ORANGE LOVE

Oranges have an amazing smell that can make you feel really good.

Make yourself an orange pomander or give it to someone else who you want to feel good. You can make any design you like on the orange – be as creative as you like.

Make sure you don't use anything you are allergic to and ask an adult to help you with this activity.

YOU WILL NEED:

Orange or tangerine

Sharp pencil

Some cloves

Metal teaspoon

Rubber bands

String or ribbon

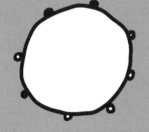

INSTRUCTIONS:

Use the edge of the teaspoon to scrape small sections of peel away, making designs in the skin of the orange. Your fingernail works well, too!

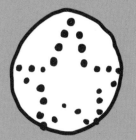

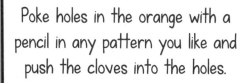

Poke holes in the orange with a pencil in any pattern you like and push the cloves into the holes.

You can experiment with star shapes, spirals, rows and zigzags.

Make designs using rubber bands or ribbons.

MILD MONSTERS

Cut out and color these frightening fear monsters.

Take away their power by trapping them in jars without oxygen, food, or water. Label the jars with their names.

Put them where you can see them every day.

Trapped in the jar, they can't grow or bother you.

When you're no longer afraid of them, just throw them in the trash and recycle the jars.

LOVE UNLIMITED

Fill this page with love for one person or thing in your life that is super special to you.

SUPERHERO

Stand in front of a mirror with your hands on your hips.

Now smile and imagine you are your very own superhero who's going to support and protect both you and others from one of your fears.

THINGS TO WORK OUT

What is your superhero name? ....

What is your superpower? ....

What fear are you fighting for the world? ....

What costume will you wear? ....

How will you change into your costume? ....

Make a mind movie, where your superhero saves the day.

You could write a newspaper report or make a TV report about it.

COURAGEOUS

BRAVE

BRAVE TIMES

WHO DO YOU DO?

Play this game with your friends and family whenever you want a good chuckle.

Take turns to impersonate an animal, a cartoon character, or a famous person you admire.

Here are some animal ideas to start you off:

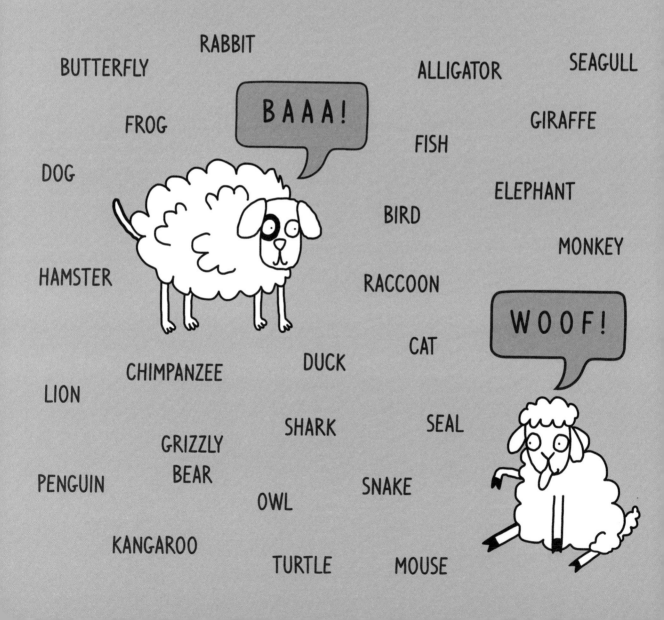

RABBIT

BUTTERFLY

ALLIGATOR

SEAGULL

FROG

BAAA!

GIRAFFE

FISH

DOG

ELEPHANT

BIRD

MONKEY

HAMSTER

RACCOON

WOOF!

CAT

CHIMPANZEE

DUCK

LION

SHARK

SEAL

GRIZZLY BEAR

PENGUIN

SNAKE

OWL

KANGAROO

TURTLE

MOUSE

LETTERS HELP

Write a letter to yourself as if it's from someone you've helped out in the past.

Imagine how it made them feel to get your support and the difference it made to them.

It doesn't need to be a big thing – even something small makes a difference to others when they are in need.

Whom did you help?   What was the problem?   What did you do?

LEAF ME ALONE

Every year, the seasons change and old leaves get blown away to make room for fresh, new leaves.

You can get rid of old, unwanted thoughts for much nicer, fresher ones.

Fill in these leaves with old worries and fears you want to get rid of and then imagine the wind blowing them away.

Now make some fresh, new
thoughts to help you feel happier.

I — TIME

Like everyone else, you need time to think about and learn to understand yourself, so you can ask for what you need.

WHEN I'M TIRED, I

get grumpy.

. . . .

I NEED

an early night.

. . . .

WHEN I'M SCARED, I

. . . .

I NEED

. . . .

WHEN

. . . .

I NEED

. . . .

WHEN

. . . .

I NEED

. . . .

WHEN

. . . .

I NEED

. . . .

WHEN I'M HAPPY, I

. . . .

I NEED

. . . .

Fill in these boxes with how you feel, or things you do when you experience different emotions, and then write down what you need in order to feel better.

WHEN

. . . .

I NEED

. . . .

WHEN

. . . .

I NEED

. . . .

WHEN I'M BORED, I

. . . .

I NEED

. . . .

WHEN

. . . .

I NEED

. . . .

WHEN

. . . .

I NEED

. . . .

WHEN I'M ANGRY, I

. . . .

I NEED

. . . .

Why not read these to someone to practice asking for help so that it's easier the next time?

WORD UP

Fill this whole page with
your favorite word or phrase.

 # ACTION!

Let's defeat one of your fears. Work out what you need to do to make it happen and whose help you need.

Make a storyboard to show what you are going to do.

TIP
Sometimes it's easier to start at the end and work backward.

How is life better without this problem?

What can you do now that you're free of this fear?

COPING TOOLBOX

There might be days
when it's hard to
BE BRAVE!

This coping toolbox will
help with remembering
how strong and amazing
you really are.

Gather some things that bring
a smile to your face that will
help you to fix your fears.

These are your tools!

To make your toolbox, find a shoebox and decorate it however you like.

Or you could use a gift box or gift bag.

Try to choose tools that help you:

Feel healthy

Feel safe

Feel loved

Feel you belong

Feel you're a good person

Feel you can achieve goals

TIP
Photos of you with family and friends, letters, birthday cards, thank-you notes, certificates, stickers, sports medals, hobby things, drawings and sticky notes are all good tools.

THE SAFE ZONE

CALM

FEAR

Find a calm, quiet spot where you can relax.

Breathe in and out deeply for three minutes. In time with your "in" breath, say in your head *"breathe in calm"* and in time with your "out" breath, say *"breathe out fear."*

Now, imagine a place where you could feel totally safe and comfortable.

Draw it with lots of detail, or stick in a picture from a magazine or a photo.

Spend five minutes staring at your picture and make a mind movie of you being there and feeling great!

Your safe place could be somewhere you've seen, been to, heard about, read about or dreamed about. It's a special safe place where everything feels peaceful, calm and secure.

SOUNDS GOOD

Whether it's noisy or quiet where you are,
take a minute to listen closely to your world.

Kick off your shoes and
socks, get comfy, close
your eyes and just listen
for a whole minute.

Try to follow the
sounds without working
out what they are or
judging them in any way.

Reckon you can do two minutes next time?
Give it a try! Increase by a minute each time, if you like.

THE BEST DAYS

Fill these album pages with your happiest memories of good times and achievements.

Label each one and tell someone all about it if you want to, or just keep it to yourself.

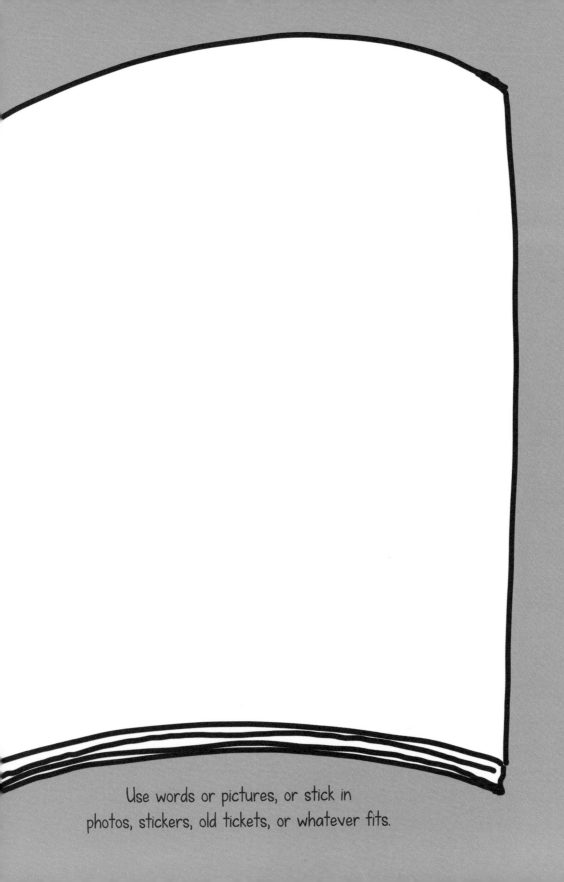

Use words or pictures, or stick in
photos, stickers, old tickets, or whatever fits.

DEAR YOU

Has someone upset you? Maybe you want to explain to one of your fears why you want it to leave you alone.

Write a letter to express what the problem is and what you want to happen next. Include your thoughts about how much better life will be without this bad feeling.

AFFIRMATIONS

I am a strong, brave, and capable person who can cope.

I can solve problems.

I think of others.

I CAN'T CONTROL WHAT OTHERS DO, BUT I CAN CONTROL MY OWN REACTIONS.

I am kind.

Think of some positive things about yourself and fill in these rays to remind yourself.

Say them out loud before you go to bed each night
and when you first wake up in the morning.

A MOMENT IN TIME

You won't always feel the same as you do right now.

Make yourself a time capsule to record how things are for you today, so you can look back to this time from the future! You could even do this each year on a date that is special to you and see what's changed.

YOU WILL NEED:

A large jar or plastic container

Plastic wrap

Collection of information about yourself, photos and memorabilia

INSTRUCTIONS:

Put your collection into the jar or container. Seal it up. Decide where you're going to store your capsule. Wrap it in plastic wrap and bury it in your backyard if you want to (ask a parent or guardian before doing this!) – don't forget to write down where it is so you can find it again!

You could record all kinds of information about yourself, such as your name, age, school, teacher or height. Maybe you'd like to include what you want to do when you grow up.

HOW ABOUT PUTTING IN A LIST OF YOUR FAVORITE THINGS:

Songs
Singers
Foods
Games
Hobbies

Toys
Books
Movies
Celebrities

Teachers
Friends
School subjects
Sports teams
Colors

LET IT GO!

Is there something you've been holding on to for a really long time?

It may be a memory, a worry, a fear or just a bad feeling.

Write down your thoughts, feelings or memories on the balloons and set them free into the sky. Watch them fly away from you forever.

Picture them disappearing over the horizon.

Now you're free to **BE BRAVE!**

Spend a minute or two visualizing yourself acting brave.

Have you ever wanted to create your own island?

What kind of a place would it be?

What would you call it?

Make a map so you know how to get around – you can invite visitors if you want to.

Make a key so you can show the landscape and features.

KEY:

RIGHT NIGHT

At bedtime, it's good to settle all three parts of your brain, so that you can sleep well and wake refreshed.

TRY THE BEDTIME ROUTINE IN THIS ORDER:

Breathe deeply and calmly for a few minutes while you're still sitting on your bed to get your turtle-brain ready for sleep.

Do triangle breathing or another technique you may know. You can do this by yourself or with someone else.

Get into bed and close your eyes for 10 seconds. Then open them again and count to 30. Repeat this three times.

Remember to keep your deep breathing going. Your mouse-brain will be snoozing in no time.

NEXT, PREPARE YOUR ME-BRAIN FOR SLEEP.
HERE'S HOW:

1
Read a book you love that will help to settle you for about 10 minutes.

2
Put the book down and then tell yourself three positive things about the day you've had.

3
Say thank you in your mind to three people who helped you today – you might be one of those people!

4
Think of three positive things you're looking forward to tomorrow.

5
Look at three things in your room that you love having near you – maybe a photo, a teddy or your favorite book.

6
Close your eyes and notice three things you can feel, like your own breathing, the softness of your duvet, or anything else.

There is nothing special about the number three, so if you prefer another number, use that instead!

COLOR THIS IN

Color this however you like.

I'M STRONGER THAN I KNOW

Now you're an expert at BE BRAVE!
Make a record here every time you overcome any
of your fears, however small or big your success.

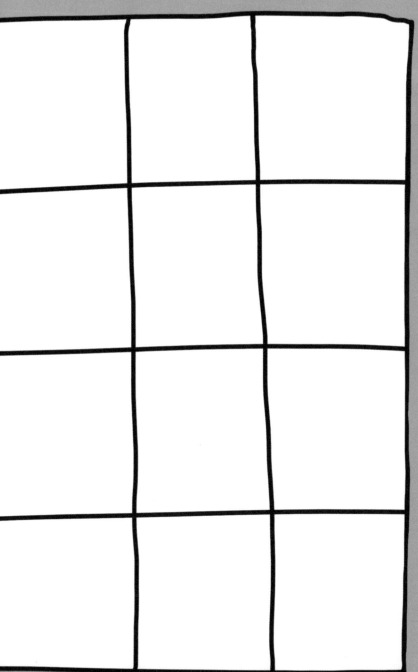

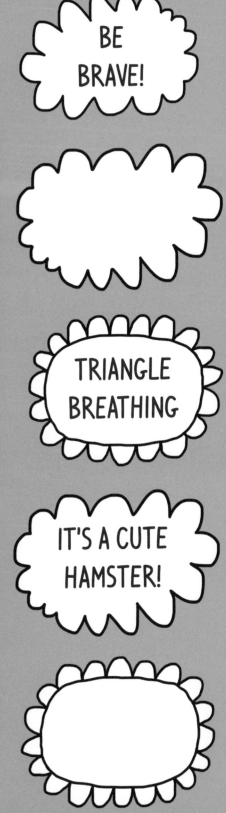

BE BRAVE!

TRIANGLE BREATHING

IT'S A CUTE HAMSTER!

TICKET TO RIDE

Design a ticket to take you somewhere peaceful and calm or maybe somewhere exciting and adventurous.

WHERE WILL YOU GO?

_____

HOW WILL YOU GET THERE?

_____

WHO WILL COME WITH YOU?

_____

_____

Remember to add your name, so everyone knows it's your ticket to wherever you want to go.

Picture the destination clearly in your mind while you make your ticket.

WHAT WILL YOU DO?

THE PAGE FOR GROWN-UPS

This activity book is perfect for parents, teachers, learning mentors, caregivers, therapists, social workers, and youth leaders who want to help children to understand and leave behind their worries.

Modern life for our children can be highly stressful. It can feel like it's all about being popular and successful. We know that they experience many internal and external pressures and can start to compare themselves with others around them and feel they aren't good enough, which may lead them to becoming fearful of everyday challenges.

Children are very resilient and, in a loving and nurturing environment, will often work through problems and difficult times without needing additional help. This book offers the chance for the child to explore, express and explain their fears and open up the conversation with you. The fun activities build resilience, increase inner calm and courage, improve understanding of emotions and encourage a positive sense of their capacity to be brave.

When children feel afraid, they may become overwhelmed and isolated and struggle to make sense of what is happening because they don't have the language or tools to explain their distress. You might notice a decline in self-esteem and confidence, along with complaints of stomachaches, headaches or feeling exhausted, and avoidance of previously enjoyed activities.

If your child's distress or fear persists beyond three months or escalates rather than decreases, you can talk to their school, a doctor or a counselor.

NATIONAL ALLIANCE ON MENTAL ILLNESS (NAMI)

Educate, advocate, listen, lead.

The NAMI HelpLine can be reached Monday through Friday, 10 am–6 pm.

NAMI is the nation's largest grassroots mental health organization dedicated to building better lives for the millions of Americans affected by mental illness.

www.nami.org

Tel: 1-800-950-NAMI (6264)
info@nami.org

GOODTHERAPY.ORG®

Helping people find therapists. Advocating for ethical therapy.

GoodTherapy.org offers a directory to help you in your search for a therapist. Using the directory, you can search by therapist location, specialization, gender, and age group treated. If you search by location, your results will include the therapists near you and will display their credentials, location, and the issues they treat.

Tel: 1-888-563-2112 ext. 1

www.goodtherapy.org

CHALLENGE THE STORM™

Sharing stories, resources and support for people facing emotional challenges.

Share your story and express yourself openly, and free from judgement.

www.challengethestorm.org

DR. SHARIE COOMBES